SCIENCE
COMICS

CORAL REEFS
Cities of the Ocean

CORAL REEFS
Cities of the Ocean

MARIS WICKS

:01

First Second
New York

and pipefish, sponges of all shapes and colors, and the tiniest little shrimp and crabs hiding inside coral branches. I love spotting the wavy arm of a brittle star poking out from a crevice or seeing a nocturnal basket star curled up into a little ball on a giant sea fan. My favorites are the nudibranchs—beautiful little shell-less snails.

As a marine scientist I've traveled to some of the most remote places on our beautiful planet, searching for healthy coral reefs. They are increasingly hard to find. As you will read in chapter 5, coral reefs are in trouble. Their problems are complicated. Just like each human is unique and can get sick from different diseases or react to illness in different ways, each reef is unique and can suffer from different problems, with different potential solutions. Luckily, there are lots of ways to help coral reefs. (Chapter 5 is full of great suggestions!) And best of all, the things that we need to do to help corals also help other organisms and ecosystems that we love: Polar bears! Rain forests! Whales! Elephants! Aye-ayes! To ensure the survival of all of these creatures, we need to preserve their habitats and keep them clean and safe. We need to protect biodiversity to maintain food sources, symbioses, habitat, and so on. In addition, we need to prevent those animals from being harvested, poached, or otherwise removed.

But what can you do if you've never even seen a coral reef? There are so many ways to help, and all of them make a difference. For example, if you live in North America, plant a milkweed. Really! It might sound weird, but let's consider it. Milkweed gives monarch butterflies a breeding habitat and a food source for their caterpillars. At the same time, milkweed plants also prevent runoff, provide a nectar source for insects, take up space that might otherwise be occupied by an invasive species, and connect people to nature. But wait a minute…can planting milkweed actually save coral reefs? Not exactly. But it's still a positive choice for our planet. Every choice you make matters. Recycling your water bottles is a good choice. Better yet, avoid all single-use plastics. Buy second-hand clothing and toys. Turn lights off when not in use. If you get into the habit of making choices with the environment in mind, you will be making our planet a better place. You make choices that impact the environment with every dollar you spend, every action you take, and every vote that you cast. A few good choices can make a huge difference. Just imagine if all of the seven billion people on earth made three positive environmental choices every day.

I hope you can get underwater and "fly" around a coral reef sometime—it's pretty amazing. But if you can't, learning about corals in this awesome comic book will help you to see just how amazing the corals and reefs that we're trying to protect are. And if you make great choices to support the environment you won't need to fly—you'll already be a superhero.

—Randi Rotjan, Ph.D.
Associate Research Scientist, New England Aquarium

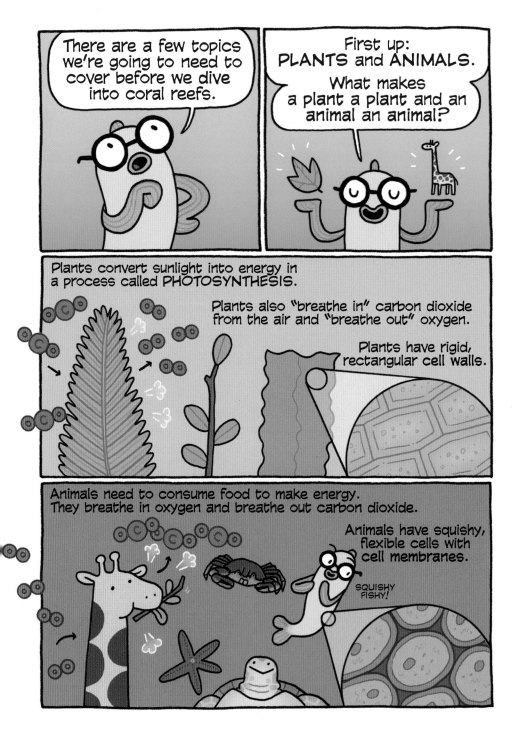

There are a few topics we're going to need to cover before we dive into coral reefs.

First up: PLANTS and ANIMALS.

What makes a plant a plant and an animal an animal?

Plants convert sunlight into energy in a process called PHOTOSYNTHESIS.

Plants also "breathe in" carbon dioxide from the air and "breathe out" oxygen.

Plants have rigid, rectangular cell walls.

Animals need to consume food to make energy. They breathe in oxygen and breathe out carbon dioxide.

Animals have squishy, flexible cells with cell membranes.

SQUISHY FISHY!

That's the author up there, talking to a dolphin.

Corals can be placed into a smaller group of invertebrates called cnidarians.*

Other notable cnidarians include:

sea pens

sea jellies

sea anemones

At a glance, they might seem very different, but a closer look will reveal some of their unifying characteristics.

Radial symmetry! Each of us has a center point (our mouth!) with a body radiating out from that point.

And we all have flexible tentacles that help us catch our prey.

Just wave your tentacles in the air!

Wave 'em like you just don't care!

Each tentacle comes equipped with thousands of microscopic stinging cells called nematocysts.

SPROING!

*Pronounced "NIE-darians"; the "C" is silent!

YEEOW!

When a tentacle comes in contact with another living thing, its nematocysts automatically eject.

Cnidarians use this adaptation to stun or kill prey before bringing it to their mouths.

YEEOW!

YEEOW!

Don't worry—cnidarians are not your nemesis.

The stinging action is involuntary; cnidarians cannot control it.

Ooops! I thought you were food!

FOOD!

The only time they will not sting is if they touch another jelly of the same species.

There, there, human.

It's nothing against you.

It's the jelly's natural reaction.

*Cnidarians don't have eyes or teeth.
Actually, some of them have very primitive eyes, called eye spots or ocelli.

8

Each polyp creates its own base as it grows...

...it builds a new base on top of the previous one.

It takes hundreds, even thousands, of generations of polyps to form this skeleton...

...and thousands, even millions, of years to form a coral reef.

Corals are colonial.

Coral polyps live together in large formations (also called corals).

The species of coral dictates the shape of the coral's skeleton.

One last coral-specific characteristic is the presence of zooxanthellae.

ZOO-OH-WHAT?

*Deep-sea/cold-water corals have different needs.

CLOSE PROXIMITY TO SUNLIGHT

Because zooxanthellae use photosynthesis, the corals must be close enough to the surface to access sunlight.

Reef-building corals are found at a depth of up to 230 feet deep, but thrive at surface level to 90 feet.

230 feet = 70.104 meters
90 feet = 27.432 meters

LIMITED TEMPERATURE RANGE

Corals have a specific range of temperatures that they can survive in: 64°–84° F (18°–28° C)

Most plants and animals on this planet have their own temperature ranges— even humans!

And we usually need some help from clothes to stay comfortable.

STEADY SALINITY (SALT) LEVELS

CHLORINE
Cl

H H
O

Ca
CALCIUM

Corals need salinity levels to remain between 30–40 parts per thousand.

MAGNESIUM
Mg

Corals will not grow in areas of the ocean near a river or other freshwater source.

Na
SODIUM

H H
O

Now that you know a bit more about coral as an animal, let's look at—

The salt in the ocean is NOT the same as table salt!

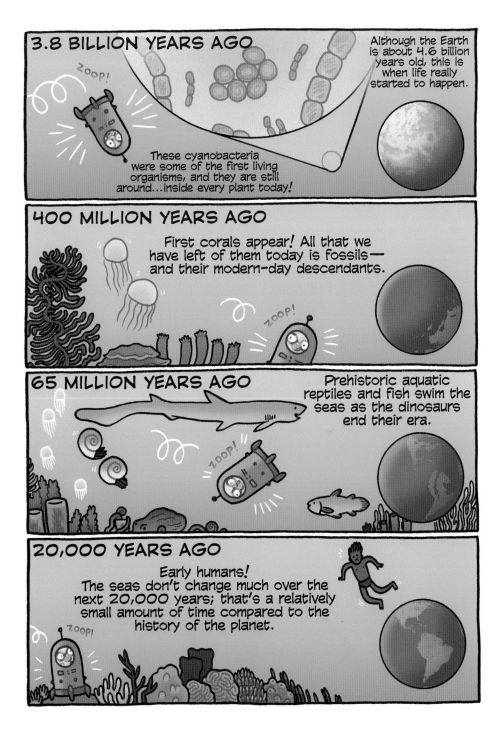

3.8 BILLION YEARS AGO

ZOOP!

Although the Earth is about 4.6 billion years old, this is when life really started to happen.

These cyanobacteria were some of the first living organisms, and they are still around...inside every plant today!

400 MILLION YEARS AGO

First corals appear! All that we have left of them today is fossils— and their modern-day descendants.

ZOOP!

65 MILLION YEARS AGO

Prehistoric aquatic reptiles and fish swim the seas as the dinosaurs end their era.

ZOOP!

20,000 YEARS AGO

Early humans! The seas don't change much over the next 20,000 years; that's a relatively small amount of time compared to the history of the planet.

ZOOP!

Plants, animals, fungi, and even viruses and bacteria have to adapt in order to survive, and not all species are that lucky...

Alas, poor T. rex, I knew him well.

Ahem, I'm looking at YOU, dinosaurs.

Many invertebrates, especially marine invertebrates, have been around for millions of years, and they've developed a number of adaptations.

Adaptations like having an exoskeleton...

...or a calcium carbonate shell...

...or stinging cells to catch food.

Even methods of reproduction can have an advantage: corals are broadcast spawners.

Here we go...

Whee!!

They all release their sperm and eggs at the same time and hope for the best.

Ooh! There! That looks like a nice place to settle down!

Still, this life cycle has many perks. Once fertilized coral eggs begin development, they seek out the most optimal place to settle.

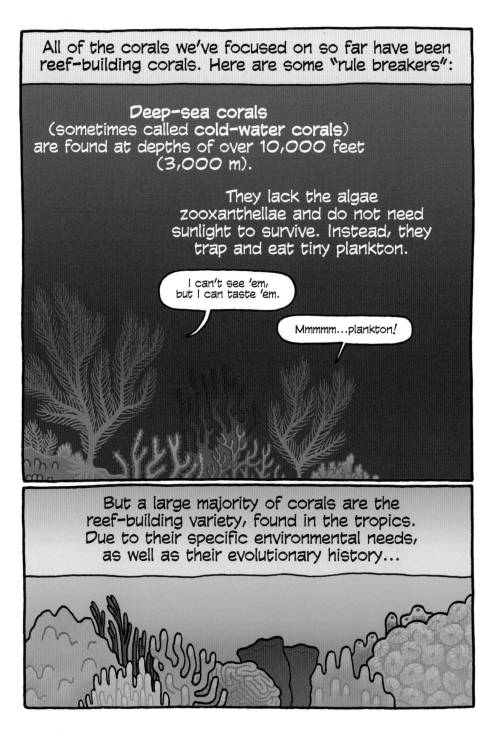

All of the corals we've focused on so far have been reef-building corals. Here are some "rule breakers":

Deep-sea corals
(sometimes called **cold-water corals**)
are found at depths of over 10,000 feet
(3,000 m).

They lack the algae zooxanthellae and do not need sunlight to survive. Instead, they trap and eat tiny plankton.

I can't see 'em, but I can taste 'em.

Mmmmm...plankton!

But a large majority of corals are the reef-building variety, found in the tropics. Due to their specific environmental needs, as well as their evolutionary history...

...coral reefs only occupy about .1% of the planet's surface.

Despite this small area of coverage, coral reefs are home to **25%** of all the animals found in the ocean.

Of the 35 major animal groups (called phyla), 32 can be found in coral reefs (versus only 9 in a rain forest*). Coral reefs are some of the greatest examples of biodiversity found on Earth.

Here are just a fraction of the animals that can be found in one square foot of a reef.

*To be fair, oceans have been around waaaaaaaaaaaaaay longer than rain forests, like BILLIONS of years longer.

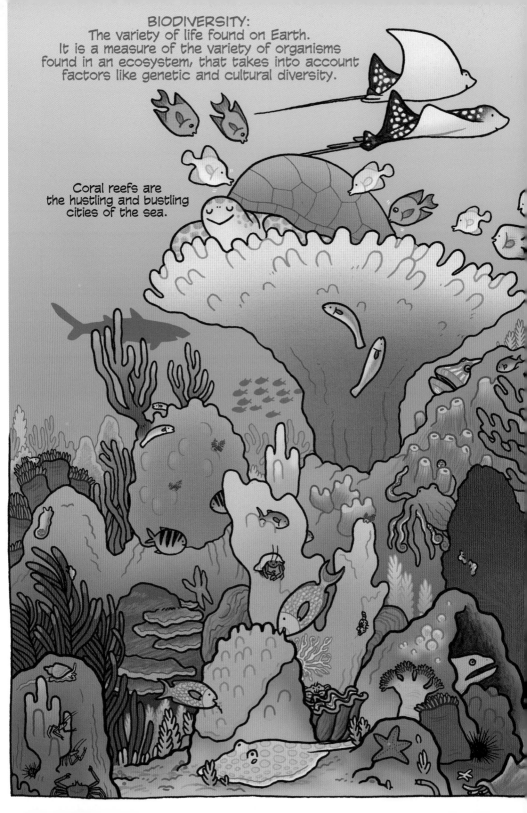

BIODIVERSITY:
The variety of life found on Earth.
It is a measure of the variety of organisms
found in an ecosystem, that takes into account
factors like genetic and cultural diversity.

Coral reefs are
the hustling and bustling
cities of the sea.

Inside each of these buildings are thousands of people...just as the outside of a coral can be home to thousands of animals.

And, just like in a city of people, there are different jobs in the reef: scavengers, predators, filter feeders.

A food web will often adapt and evolve with the reef itself, sustaining a balanced habitat for the residents.

Food webs aren't just found in coral reefs! Every animal on this planet fits into a food web, it just depends on where they live, what they eat, and who eats them. Whether you live...

...in the Arctic

the Deep Sea

freshwater

or even on land!

Coral reefs aren't just a habitat and food source for the animals that live there, they are also a food source or livelihood for over 1 BILLION human beings!

Even though coral reefs cover less than .1% of the Earth's surface, the number of animals that depend on them for food and shelter is HUGE.

Coral reefs play a large role in global ocean health.

But first let's get up close and personal with some of their inhabitants...

CHAPTER THREE:
THE CORAL REEF
ECOSYSTEM
EXPLORED!

We've looked at a lot of general coral reef information so far: what type of animals corals are, what is their life cycle, how reefs are formed, where they are found...

Now we're going to examine specific species of corals, as well as many other animals that inhabit reefs.

All the information in this book comes from research!

Data collected by scientists from hundreds of years ago has shaped our knowledge of the world around us (and above us and below us).

Studying the information that has already been researched paves the way for future research and future scientists.*

Before we highlight individual species...

...let's take a look at the system we use to categorize animals (and plants and fungi and so on).

*Like you! YOU may be a future scientist!

KINGDOM

I belong to ANIMALIA!

Other kingdoms include Plantae, Fungi, and a bunch of teeny tiny stuff.*

PHYLUM

There are 35 phyla (that's the plural of "phylum") in kingdom Animalia...

I belong to Chordata!

(And so do YOU!)

CLASS

Now that we're narrowing it down, everyone is starting to look a bit more similar. All fish with bony skeletons fall into the same class:

Osteichthyes!

ORDER

There are over 45 different orders of bony fish, but I am proud to call myself:

Perciformes.

FAMILY

Ha! It's a like a family reunion in here! A family reunion of **Gobiidae**, that is...

GENUS

Okay, now we're down to my CLOSEST relatives: *Cryptocentrus*

...and SPECIES

cinctus!

Cryptocentrus cinctus, to be exact. As a rule, GENUS and SPECIES are always written together (in *italics*, with SPECIES all lowercase).

But you can call me a yellow prawn-goby if that's easier; it's my common name.

*Bacteria, Archaea, and Protista—and, despite their teeny tininess, they are all very important!

33

Montastraea cavernosa
Great Star Coral

Mound and boulder
corals are some of the
chief reef builders.

This species can grow
to 5 feet (1.5 m)
in diameter!

Orbicella faveolata
Mountainous Star Coral

The mountainous
star coral can get
even bigger—up to
30 feet (10 m)
across and 15 feet
(5 m) high.

Siderastrea siderea
Starlet Coral

Another massive coral,
starlet coral can grow to be
up to 6 feet (2 m) wide.

Diploria strigosa
Symmetrical Brain Coral

This coral can grow to be almost 6 feet (1.8 m) in diameter.

Diploria labyrinthiformis
Grooved Brain Coral

Have you figured out why we're called "brain" coral yet?

Mussa angulosa
Spiny Flower Coral

Each of these circles are individual polyps!

Acropora palmata
Elkhorn Coral

This coral is another big reef builder.

Branching corals grow faster than mound and boulder corals.

Porites furcata
Branched Finger Coral

Sadly, there is no "Toe Coral."

Madracis mirabilis
Yellow Pencil Coral

While the short branches are small, the whole colony of this coral can reach several feet (or meters) in diameter.

Pencil Coral is not to be used as a writing utensil.

39

Montipora aequituberculata
Encrusting Pore Coral

This coral grows
in plates and can
cover huge portions
of a reef.

Agaricia fragilis
Fragile Saucer Coral

Fragile saucer coral* can
be found under ledges and
on the tops of reefs.

Tubastraea coccinae
Orange Cup Coral

Cup corals are
actually non-reef building, and
don't even have zooxanthellae,
but they can be found in both
deep, cold water and shallow,
warm water.

*Not to be confused with "flying saucer coral."

GORGONIANS
(aka Sea Whips or Sea Fans)

I'm a big fan...
of being a
gorgonian!

Gorgonians are
closely related to corals,
and can be found
branching out on reefs
all over the world.

Har. Har.
Sea puns.

Millepora alcicornis
Branching Fire Coral

STOP!!

This is not actually
a coral; it is a hydroid!
Hydroids are more closely
related to jellies, and live in
large groups called colonies.
But even more important—
they STING. A LOT.

Thanks for clearing that up...
now come closer so I can
STING YOU!!

And that's just a handful of the over 6,000 known coral species!

Let's meet some of the other nautical cnidarians.

SEA ANEMONES

Anemones can be found all over the reef, catching small prey with their stinging cells.

Some fish have adapted to live IN the anemone—they have a layer of mucus that protects them from stings.

SEA JELLIES

This is kind of an umbrella term for anything in the ocean that is alive and jellylike.

YAH!

I'm a sea wasp (aka box jelly, aka Cubozoan). I've been called one of the mostly deadly stingers on the planet.

Portuguese man-o'-war here. I'm actually a colony of hydroids!

I'm a moon jelly, and my stinging cells are so tiny, they can't even sting humans.*

*Even though this is true, it's still a good idea to NEVER touch a jelly.

43

PHYLUM: Platyhelminthes

You can just call us "flatworms"...

...and we are FABULOUS.

Coral reefs are home to a plethora of colorful platyhelminthes.*

PHYLUM: Annelidae

I like to catch prey with my venomous jaws!

I like to catch plankton with my bristles!

I filter-feed like the feather dusters!

Clam Worm

Feather Duster Worm

Christmas Tree Worm

*Not featured are parasitic flatworms, like the 100-plus feet one that is found inside whales' intestines!

PHYLUM: Echinodermata

eyespot

mouth

tube feet

arm

anus

water pump

gills

spines

Sea Stars

Five-point radial symmetry, spiny skin, and a central mouth are all unifying characteristics of echinoderms.

Sea Urchins

spines

We weren't kidding around with the "spiny" thing.

spines

mouth

With our mouths on our bottoms, whatever we are sitting on, we're eating. We're like little coral reef vacuum cleaners.

spines

Sand dollars are actually a type of sea urchin.

Many molluscs are a bit...sluggish when it comes to moving.

Flamingo Tongue Snail

I live on soft corals like this gorgonian and eat the fleshy part of the coral. Mmmm-mm-mmm.

My shell is actually cream-colored; it's my soft mantle (body) that gives me these fantastic markings.

om nom nom

Queen Conch

Kneel before me, loyal subjects!!

Despite my large size, I am actually a herbivore. My diet consists of algae; I am another vacuum cleaner of the reef. But a royal vacuum cleaner.

Cone Snail

I am one of the most DEADLY animals in the world; my venom is strong enough to kill even the biggest animal. But I use it to kill my prey...which happens to be small fish.

I deliver my venom via a built-in harpoon.

Hah! You're just a snail—

AHHHHHH

harpoon'd!

Cuttlefish

I inhabit the bottom of reefs, snacking on shrimp and small fish.

CLASS: Cephalopods

Although I appear to have no shell, inside my body is a cuttlebone. It's like an inner shell made of calcium carbonate (the same thing coral skeletons are made of!).

Oh yeah! And all of us cephalopods can change the color and texture of our skin!

Octopus

I'm another bottom-dwelling, tentacled tenant of the reef.

I catch crabs and bring them into my mouth, where I chomp them up with my beak.

Squid

We are open-water, nocturnal reef swimmers!

We snack on other nighttime swimmers like small fish and krill.

And the award for best camouflage goes to...THESE DUDES.

PHYLUM: Arthropoda

All of us arthropods have a hard outer shell called an exoskeleton.

We also have segmented bodies and jointed limbs.

Channel Clinging Crab

I am a cleaner shrimp; I wave at fish passing by with my antennae.

When they stop, I crawl on them (and even inside their mouths!) to clean off any dead skin or parasites.

You could say that I'm sort of like the car wash of the reef...if you think of the fish as cars.

Banded Coral Shrimp

Arrow Crab

I can often be found hiding in anemones, and I'm mostly active at night.

I like to feast on feather duster worms and other reef invertebrates.

BEEP BEEP make way for the fishmobile!

Hermit Crab

How do you like my shell? It's an old snail shell. Us hermit crabs are the ultimate recyclers of the reef.

All arthropods grow larger by molting: we grow a new exoskeleton under our current one, and we shed our old exoskeleton.

When my exoskeleton gets too big for my snail shell home, I have to find a new, empty shell to move into.

Spiny Lobster

I eat other small invertebrates that live in the reef.

I don't have large claws to protect myself. Instead, I rub my antennae against my body, which makes a loud SCREEEEECH sound.

Slipper Lobster

I'm a bottom dweller of coral reefs. My heavily armored exoskeleton protects me from most predators.

I snack on the small invertebrates I find on the ground.

Despite my name, I am not suitable to be worn on the feet of humans.

So don't even think about it.

57

BONY FISH! (That's me!)

Also called Osteichthyes, us bony fish all have a skeleton made of bone, a body covered in scales, and one gill slit with a cover called an operculum.

Just as we saw variety in the diet, body shape, and behavior of the sharks and rays, there are some pretty...interesting characters in the bony fish family.

There is one group of fishes that make up a whopping **25%** of the whole reef fish population—GOBIES! (Again, that's ME!)

Full of yourself much?

Well, I AM the narrator.

Parrotfish

There are over 90 different species of parrotfish found in coral reefs all over the world.

I happen to be a rainbow parrotfish.

I can thank my brilliantly colored scales for that name...

MUNCH MUNCH

Mmmm...I've got a sharp beaklike mouth that I use to scrape at algae on the reef.

Some types of parrotfish even eat coral polyps; we're like the garden pruners of the reef.

Barracuda

Barracudas are some of the largest (and, in my tiny opinion, scariest) fish in the reef. Their V-shaped tail and slender body mean that they are fast swimmers.

It's impolite to talk with your mouth full, Mr. Moray.

ORDER: Reptilia

All reptiles are cold-blooded* and have scales.

There are 7 species of sea turtles found on Earth, and many of them can be found in coral reefs in both the Atlantic and Indo-Pacific Oceans.

Sea turtles spend their lives swimming all over the ocean (and world!), but the coral reef is just as important to them as the open ocean.

Reefs provide two valuable resources: a place to rest...

Z

...and a place to eat.

*With one exception: the leatherback sea turtle can regulate its body temperature!

ORDER: Mammalia
Dolphins

We're another apex predator found near coral reefs. We feast on squid, crabs, and small fish.

All habitats need big eaters like us to keep the food web in balance.

There's one more mammal that can often be found in and around coral reefs...

...HUMANS!

So majestic.

The ecosystems that coral reefs sustain provide food and jobs to millions and millions of people... and beyond!

In addition to food, jobs, and tourism...

...coral reefs are a natural barrier that protect the coast.

Thanks!

No prob!

Reefs also maintain a calm, shallow area of ocean that fosters a safe place for animals to mate and give birth, sustaining the food web.

It's easy to see how humans living near reefs are affected by them...

...but what about someone who lives thousands of miles away from a coral reef?

?

To see this connection, we must look at the oceans (and land) on a **global** level:

Oh right; you're zoomed out already...

You can come a little closer.

We've looked at coral reef ecosystems, but let's go BIG and look at the global ecosystem, starting with...

WATER

Hi again!

Without water, we would not have life on Earth.

After all, humans are roughly **60%** water!

Water pants!

(Not a realistic representation; water is distributed throughout my cells and tissues, thankyouverymuch.)

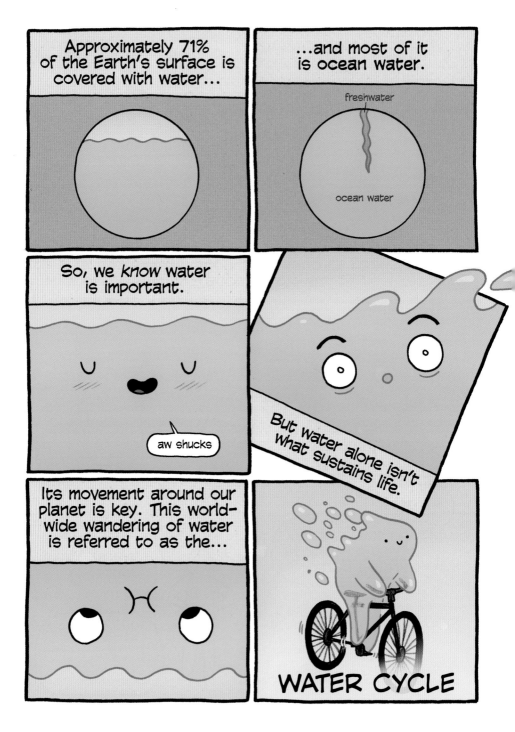

Approximately 71% of the Earth's surface is covered with water...

...and most of it is ocean water.

freshwater

ocean water

So, we know water is important.

aw shucks

But water alone isn't what sustains life.

Its movement around our planet is key. This world-wide wandering of water is referred to as the...

WATER CYCLE

The sun heats water on the surface (primarily ocean water, but also lakes, ponds, rivers, even puddles).

Water molecules rise, or evaporate, in the form of water vapor.

The water vapor condenses to form clouds; air currents move these clouds all over the planet.

As the clouds become more dense, water drops form and fall to Earth.

This is called precipitation.

This water either infiltrates the ground or travels along the surface.

*With the exception of icy comets that have previously collided with the Earth.

For a long time, humans assumed that trees and plants were responsible for the world's oxygen production.

Trees do help, but they only supply the earth with about 30-40% of its oxygen...no offense, trees!

None taken!

After all, we only cover about 8% of the Earth's surface.

To find our main producers of oxygen, grab your microscope and head out into the ocean.

*This is the number of people that DIRECTLY depend on the ocean.

*Or, like, any clothes at all. Because fish don't wear clothes.

It also means that you have to dress differently for each season.

BRRRR

Mmm... much better.

Sometimes the terms climate and weather are confused.

Weather is what happens day to day...

Hmm, what to wear.

...while climate describes year-to-year patterns.

Oof! Time to put away my winter clothes and bring out my summer ones!

SUMMER CLOTHES

One hot day in the winter or one cold day in the summer doesn't mean the climate is changing...

pff

...but seeing an increase in warming or an increase in cooling over 30 or more years does.

And we've seen a steady increase in temperature over the past 200 years!

TEMP

YEAR

But the major sources of CO_2 in the past 150 years have been from human inventions.

Our planet already has ways of managing CO_2 levels thanks to phytoplankton, algae, and trees, but too much CO_2 upsets the balance.

Burning fossil fuels like coal and gas releases carbon dioxide into the atmosphere.

As carbon dioxide builds up, it creates a gassy blanket around Earth.

This thick blanket around Earth traps heat.

And all that trapped heat warms up the oceans.

This causes the global temperature to rise, having a negative impact on ecosystems that are accustomed to very slow environmental changes.

Melting polar ice, droughts, and sea level rise are just a few of the dangers from climate change.

Well, this can't be good.

Yeah, definitely NOT GOOD.

We've been looking at how climate change affects the whole planet...

Let's shift our focus to how it affects coral reefs.

CORAL BLEACHING

Remember that symbiotic relationship the corals had with the tiny algae, zooxanthellae?

And that some coral reefs have taken more that 30 million years to form?

Because of these preexisting conditions, a temperature change as little as 1 degree can upset the balance that has been long-established by the reef.

The zooxanthellae can only thrive in a specific temperature range. If it gets too hot, too fast, they become stressed and leave.

This is called "coral bleaching" because the corals lose their color when the zooxanthellae leave.

If the temperature resumes to previous levels within a short amount of time, the zooxanthellae may return.

If not, the corals can live for a while, but they will not be healthy; they may eventually die.

Changes in light and access to nutrients can also cause coral bleaching, but temperature is the most likely candidate.

OCEAN ACIDIFICATION

This is a danger for not just corals, but ANY animal in the ocean that has a shell.

When CO_2 levels increase, the ocean compensates by absorbing more CO_2 to maintain balance.

Too much CO_2 and it actually alters the chemistry of the ocean.

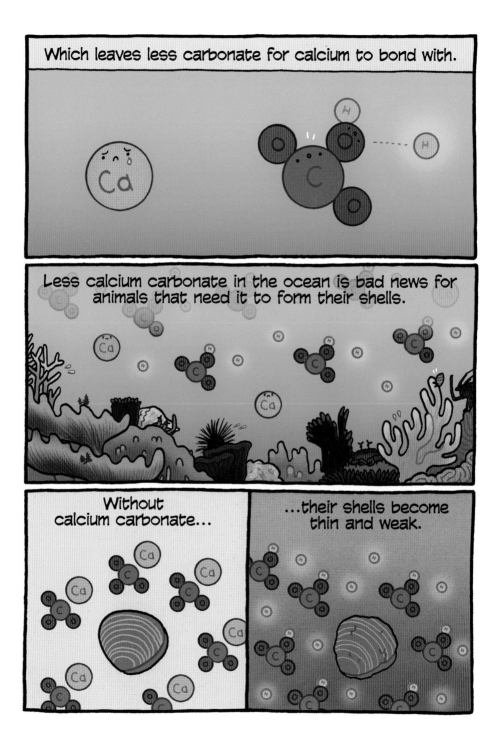

Which leaves less carbonate for calcium to bond with.

Less calcium carbonate in the ocean is bad news for animals that need it to form their shells.

Without calcium carbonate...

...their shells become thin and weak.

A weakened shell means:

Less protection from predators.

CHOMP!

Less support if your shell is part of a larger structure.

More succeptibilty to damage.

You don't have to be a chemist to see that this is bad news for any shell-making animal in the ocean.

So we know that too much carbon dioxide is bad for our planet, but what can we do?

Plastics are made from oil; more oil means more CO_2 in the atmosphere.

Use a reusable water bottle, lunch box, or snack bag to reduce the amount of plastic in your life.

Even better—get your school or house to be "zero waste" by starting a recycling and composting plan!

COMPOST (ORGANIC WASTE)

Get outside! Having fun outdoors helps us appreciate our awesome planet!

Plant a tree, participate in a trail or beach cleanup...

...or organize your own event for your friends and family!

WOO-HOO!

The notion of a fish needing a water bottle is pretty funny.

That's actually pretty good writing for a fish.

Scientists have long turned to the natural world to help find cures and treatments for human illnesses.

And coral reefs have been helping for quite some time!

All living things on this planet have similar ways that they survive. By studying the immune systems of other animals, humans can help better understand and strengthen their own.

Corals produce chemicals called secosteroids that protect them against disease.

Glad I could be of service!

Scientists have researched secosteroids and found that they can treat asthma and arthritis.

Tiny bryozoans were found to contain a substance that helps fight cancer!

Cyanobacteria (blue-green algae) is also used in cancer treatments.

Humans are great at building things, but it certainly doesn't hurt to take a look at how animals and plants create structures and support.

When people design things inspired by nature, it's called biomimicry. We've been borrowing ideas from the world around us for a long time.

Corals' calcium carbonate base is SUPER-strong and made from just a few ingredients. (H_2O, Ca, CO_2)

Engineers had an idea: Can we make a SUPER-strong cement the same way?

YES! Yes, you can!

By combining seawater and excess CO_2 from a factory, calcium carbonate is formed and processed to be made into cement.

Thanks, coral!

Bonus points for recycling waste (CO_2) from a factory...way to go, humans!

Innovation is an awesome human trait. Looking for new, more efficient ways to produce, build, and manufacture means a better planet for people...and every other living thing that calls Earth home.

Coral reefs are home to over 25% of all the animals found in the ocean.
And many of these reef inhabitants have inspired human inventions.

BEEP BEEP

The body shape of a trunkfish helped humans to design a more aerodynamic, fuel-efficient car.

Sharks' skin is covered in tiny, scale-like plates called dermal denticles.
They provide the shark with protection and also make it more hydrodynamic in the water.

Bathing suits worn by Olympic swimmers use a similar design. The same shark technology may someday cover the bottom of boats to make them faster and more efficient.

An underwater robot inspired by the shape and movement of a cuttlefish could help humans to explore parts of the ocean that are difficult to access.

BEEP BOOP

These are all examples of biomimicry!

Also, robots are just plain cool.

The author had never seen a coral reef until she started researching this book!

So. Many. Thanks.

—GLOSSARY—

Adaptation
A change (or process of change) that helps an organism better survive in its habitat

Atom
The smallest unit of matter

Biodiversity
The variety of living organisms found in a habitat/ecosystem

Biology
The study of living organisms

Calcium carbonate
A molecule that helps form mollusk shells and hard corals

Carbon dioxide
A gas that is important to plant life when it is at its natural levels; it is also a by-product of industry (factories, cars, buses, trucks, planes)

Climate
The weather in an area, over a long period of time

Ecology
The study of the interactions of living organisms and their environment over space and time

Ecosystem
A community of organisms and their interaction with their environment

Environment
The surrounding area in which a person, plant, or animal lives

Evolution
The process by which living organisms have developed and changed over time

Exoskeleton
The hard external covering for the body in some invertebrates (like a lobster's shell)

Habitat
The place where an organism lives

Invertebrate
> An animal that does not have a backbone

Life cycle
> The series of changes in the life of an organism (birth, growth, reproduction, death)

Molecule
> A group of atoms bonded together

Nematocyst
> Specialized stinging cell found in the tentacles of jellies, anemones, and corals

Organism
> A living thing (plant, animal, fungi, bacteria, etc.)

Oxygen
> A gas found in the air that supports most organisms found on Earth

Phytoplankton
> Plant plankton

Plankton
Organisms (often small or microscopic) that drift or float in the open water

Reproduction
The process by which organisms produce offspring

Salinity
The amount of salt in a body of water

Skeleton
An internal or external framework of bone, cartilage, or other hard material that supports or contains the body of a plant or animal

Vertebrate
An animal that has a backbone

Water cycle
The process by which water moves around the earth's oceans, atmosphere, and land

Zooplankton
Animal plankton

—BIBLIOGRAPHY—

General Coral Reef Information

National Oceanic and Atmospheric Administration. "NOAA's Coral Reef Conservation Program." May 7, 2015. coralreef.noaa.gov

United States Environmental Protection Agency. "Coral Reef Protection: What Are Coral Reefs?" May 14, 2015. water.epa.gov/type/oceb/habitat/coral_index.cfm

Woods Hole Oceanographic Institution. "Coral." May 7, 2015. www.whoi.edu/main/topic/coral

Marine Species Identification Portal. May 7, 2015. http://species-identification.org

Conservation and Environmental Statistics

United States Environmental Protection Agency. "Wastes: Resource Conservation: Common Wastes and Materials." May 7, 2015. www.epa.gov/epawaste//conserve/materials/index.htm

United States Environmental Protection Agency. "Climate Change." May 7, 2015. www.epa.gov/climatechange

Pacific Marine Environmental Laboratory. "What Is Ocean Acidification?" May 7, 2015. www.pmel.noaa.gov/co2/story/What+is+Ocean+Acidification

Coral Reef Technology and Innovation

Salazar, Jorge. Earthsky.org. "Brent Constantz Builds Cement Like Corals Do." May 7, 2015. earthsky.org/human-world/brent-constantz-builds-cement-like-coral-do

ETH Zurich. Sepios: Nautical Robot. May 7, 2015. sepios.org

Levins, Nicole. The Nature Conservancy. "Ocean and Coasts: Coral Reefs: Nature's Medicine Cabinet." May 7, 2015. www.nature.org/ourinitiatives/habitats/oceanscoasts/explore/coral-reefs-and-medicine.xml

Quio, Charles Q. Popular Mechanics. "Shark Skin Will Inspire Faster Swimsuits and Airplanes." May 7, 2015. www.popularmechanics.com/science/animals/a10567/shark-skin-will-inspire-faster-swimsuits-and-airplanes-16792156

—ADDITIONAL RESOURCES—

Web

Phoenix Islands Protected Area. phoenixislands.org

Smithsonian Ocean Portal. "Corals and Coral Reefs." ocean.si.edu/corals-and-coral-reefs

Wired.com. "Interactive Coral Reef Panoramas." wired.com/2013/10/coral-reef-panoramas

National Geographic. "10 Things You Can Do To Help Save The Ocean." ocean.nationalgeographic.com/ocean/take-action/10-things-you-can-do-to-save-the-ocean

Books

Coral Reef: 24 Hours. Dorling Kindersley Children. 2005.

Cole, Brandon. *Reef Life: A Guide to Tropical Marine Life*. Firefly Books, 2013.

Knowlton, Nancy. *Citizens of the Sea: Wondrous Creatures From the Census of Marine Life*. National Geographic, 2010.

A great big fishy thanks to Casey, Calista, Danielle, and the rest of the First Second family. Without them, this book wouldn't be possible.

Another great big fishy thanks to the New England Aquarium, and all of my incredible coworkers. And to the wonderful folks at Boston Scuba. I think it's also safe to say that without them, this book wouldn't be possible.

Yet another great big fishy thanks to Rosemary, Sylvia, and (especially) Casey Z.; their feedback helped build the calcium carbonate base of this book.

I hope this book inspires you to get outside and have fun in nature, whether you live right on the beach, or 2,000 miles from one.